This Journal Belongs To:

Made in United States
Troutdale, OR
06/12/2024

20493353R00066